IT NEVER HAPPENED

Peace of Christ Love!
Dorothy A. Smith

AuthorHouse™
1663 Liberty Drive
Bloomington, IN 47403
www.authorhouse.com
Phone: 1-800-839-8640

Published by AuthorHouse 12/14/2011

ISBN: 978-1-4685-2306-5 (sc)

Library of Congress Control Number: 2011962512

authorHOUSE®

IT NEVER HAPPENED

Fictional Animal Stories of Rescue

by

Dorothy A. Smith

Sketches by
Anne Turner

CONTENTS

"God bless the out stretched hands
that reach out toward preserving,
to protect, to spare His creatures,
in a manner that's deserving."

From "Ode to Animal Lovers"

By Dorothy A. Smith

ENDORSEMENTS

These animal stories are different. They hold a message about kindness. I felt as if I was right there experiencing life with these characters. It Never Happened is a great read for all ages.
- Calamity Jo of "Calamity Jo's Comedy Animal Variety Show" from the Southwest Desert of Arizona

A charming mix of real animals in their native habitat involved in fictional story situations. Ms. Smith obviously does her research and her characters make the animals come alive for the reader.
- Cheryl Simanek, MA., Midwestern University, Downers Grove, IL

A teacher for many years, Dorothy Smith knows what kids like and need. Her interesting information and lively stories appeal to a wide range of readers. I highly recommend It Never Happened.
- Jean Coulson, retired Elementray Teacher, Comptche, CA

Who among us does not love and appreciate stories about animals and their habitats? Here is a beautiful collection of fiction and fact blended to perfection in order to teach, inform and entertain both children and adults. You will enjoy these amazing adventures.
- Vivian Shavin, retired teacher, current Library Aide, Beecher, IL

It Never Happened, wins my energetic endorsement. The writer is a gifted storyteller, in fact, I refer to her as A Teacher-by-Parable. The stories are not real, but they are almost believable, and the facts are quite enriching.
- Paul Pruchnicki, retired Secondary Teacher, Bourbonnais, IL

KIDS OPINE

The zebra story, Zip Zap a Young Zebra in Kenya, was the best story about zebras that I ever read. I especially liked the part where the boys want to train a three-legged hyena to tend the sheep. I wonder if they did it.
   - David O'Keefe, 5th grade

 These stories hold high interest. Besides being a reading choice for older students they would be a treat to read aloud at Story Time for younger students. They are real attention keepers.
   - Logan Reed, 11th grade

I love panda bears, the stuffed ones, but Pip Perri Panda in China taught me so much that I never knew before. I still love panda bears but in a different way. This story was like a Fairytale I can't forget.
   - Grace Cunningham, 5th grade

This book is entertaining, informative and instructive. It is a good combination. I love being entertained when I read. I really was entertained. You'll just have to read it.
   - Michael St. Aubin, 5th grade

Zip Zap a Young Zebra in Kenya was by far my most favorite of these stories. From the telling of how the harems come together, to the love those two brothers showed, was a marvelous read.
   - Annie Mae Boarini, 8th grade

Erin and Elora, Two Great White Egrets in Tasmania was different and interesting because birds aren't used in many stories.
   - Patrick Boarini, 8th grade

Mee-Ca and Mel-Ca, Two Green Monkeys on Bardados was most interesting when Mel-Ca went out on an adventure and got his tail bitten off by a mongoose. Thankfully, he was rescued by Mr. Dewey.
   - Michael Joe Boarini, 9th grade

DEDICATION

With love I dedicate these stories to my children, grand children, great grand children, and to my nieces and nephews and their children. That number comes to 97. I could simply say, "All those who call me Grammy and Aunt Dorothy, these stories are for your enjoyment." Remember, whatever we accomplish in life eventually touches the whole family in some way.

ACKNOWLEDGEMENTS

With pleasure I include a big THANK YOU

- to Annie and David Turner for all of your valuable help in fine tuning pages, and for your health spa that was conducive to my creativity;

- to Annie, for your generous sharing of time discussing the stories, and I'm proud and grateful for your artistic rendition of the animals;

- to friends and family members I have appreciated your encouragement;

- to the host of wonderful people who rendered their critiques and worthy suggestions: Ann Blantin, Gloria Blantin, Diane Covert, Georgia Frey, Mary Jane Hodge, and Cheryl Simanek;

- to Jenna Yaeger for her CD on Zebras from her mission to Kenya;

- to the enthusiastic children who contributed their opinions to "Kids Opine" Annie Mae, Michael Joe, and Patrick Boarini, Logan Reed, Grace Cunningham, David O'Keefe, and Michael St. Aubin;

- to the distinguished people who wrote endorsements, Jeannie Coulson, Giovanna Cardella, Paul Pruchnicki, Vivian Shavin, and Cheryl Simanek.

- to Chris Toring, my Check In Coordinator at Author House, and the hard working members of the publishing staff that turned my endeavor into a finished product.

MEE-CA AND MEL-CA

TWO GREEN MONKEYS ON BARBADOS

Once upon an island called Bardados, located in the Eastern Caribbean Sea, there were two special little Green Monkeys. There names were Mee-Ca , the girl monkey, and Mel-Ca, the boy monkey. They were brother and sister, born in the Barbados Zoo. When they were born they looked bluish and had very little fur, but before they were a year old they were growing thick, brownish-grey looking fur with yellow and olive green flicks of color in it. In the sunlight they appeared greenish. That is why they are called Green Monkeys.

They are small, even when full grown they weigh about eight to ten pounds. They look like they are wearing a black mask with black ears, and they have round black eyes. Their chest has white fur and the inside fur on their legs is also white. They have a long., skinny tail that curls around their body when they want it to. The tail is quite strong and very handy for swinging and hanging in odd positions and this they love to do.

The zoo was a good home for all of the animals. Every effort was taken to keep the zoo home as close to the island living as possible. There were beautiful trees and plants, waterfalls and rock pits with iron railings surrounding them, and walkways where tourist observed the animals. The animals never had to go looking for their food. The tropical fruits and vegetables were brought to them throughout the day, everyday. Life was peaceful in the zoo.

Over three hundred and fifty years ago, the Green Monkeys were brought to Barbados from Africa. They came with the slaves who were brought over to work the sugar cane fields. The monkeys were an annoyance, wild and destructive to crops, vegetation and property. Once the zoo was built and many of the monkeys were brought to the habitat a type of order was maintained. Other animals and birds were also given a new home in the zoo. Critically endangered animals like the Red-footed Tortoise, the Hawksbill Turtle and the Leatherback Turtle were given special consideration when their eggs were due to hatch. Yes, life was peaceful in the zoo.

Mr. Dewey was one of the zoo keepers. He was popular with the animals and frequent visitors because of his friendly, compassionate temperament. Visitors remember the Tee- shirts he created for the zoo attendants like the one they wore at feeding time that had this message in big letters, "ENOUGH IS AS GOOD AS A FEAST".

One day when Mr. Dewey came into the monkey pit, he neglected to lock the gate. Mel-Ca squeezed out through the opening and wandered away. Only Mee-Ca noticed. She began to screech and chase around. The Mr. Dewey paid very little attention to her. He called out,"Hello! Mee-Ca!" and kept right on making his rounds, checking on things, and he whistled a happy tune to drown out Mee-Ca's voice.

Mee-Ca ran along the high rocks and she could see Mel-Ca swinging through the trees. He could hear her warnings, but he kept going. Then he disappeared from her sight. She paced back and forth, back and forth, screeching without stop. Soon other animals joined in ranting with her. They were stirred up getting rowdy and louder. So Mr. Dewey decided to deliver their food to the feeding spots a little earlier. They all ate except for Mee-Ca. She would not stop screeching. Soon there were tears in her eyes. Mr. Dewey grew concerned when he did not see Mel-Ca, and planned to search for him when he finished filling the food and water troughs.

Meanwhile, Mel-Ca was off on an adventure. He didn't feel lonely because of the chatter, and warbling of the many, many birds that he was disturbing as he swung and lobbed from tree to tree. He managed to pull some green bananas from a tree and ate them with hands full of wild berries. When the aching came from eating so much he curled up on a broad branch of a bamboo tree with his arms and tail wrapped around his aching stomach. He could not find comfort so he climbed down and sat resting against a tree. He moaned and moaned.

While he rested a strange looking, furry, little creature, very fast moving, kept racing around him. It was a Mongoose. The Mongooses were brought to Barbados from India by the early settlers to rid the island of the rats and snakes that destroyed crops. That was hundreds of years ago. Well, they did get rid of the big snakes like the poisonous Cobra. Many small snakes like the Thread snake, the Blind snake, the Flowerpot snake and the Racer snake still remained and are good for the soil. However, the rat population continued to grow because the Mongooses slept through the night while the rats roamed through the sugar cane. The Mongooses also raided and devoured eggs of the Green Turtle and the Leatherback Turtle after they buried them in the sandy beaches. This increased the level of endangerment for these turtles.

The Mongoose is a catlike animal, with a long narrow, hairy body with long whiskers on its face. He does not bother with humans, just their pets and trash, and he is an illegal in most countries today, however, Hawaii has a fairly large population of them and they hunt for snakes in the sugar cane fields. They don't catch the rats there either.

Mel-Ca thought the Mongoose wanted to play, but he was wrong. The Mongoose pounced on Mel-Ca's tail and began to chomp on it. Mel-Ca screeched wildly and tried to pull away, but his attacker had a strong grip on the tail, He chewed and pulled and Mel-Ca tugged and screeched non-stop as he flipped flopped on the ground. Mel-Ca gave one strong pull and fell into a clump of bushes. Half of his tail was missing.

While the Mongoose was swallowing what came off in his mouth, Mel-Ca leaped to a tree and scampered close to the top. When he looked down the Mongoose was gone. What was left of Mel-Ca's tail was quite sore and he held it up to his mouth to lick the pain away and to pout with angry screeches.

From the high branches of the tree Mel-Ca could see the beautiful blue-green ocean. He became anxious to get closer. He swung to another branch and when his tail would not curl he fell to the ground screeching in pain. Poor Mel-Ca.

He picked himself up and hurried toward the big blue-green ocean. He could hear the faint, shrill sounds of the Terns, sea birds, that circled above the water looking for fish. They were on their own mission and totally ignored him. He saw the long legged Sandpipers wadding in the water. He waited and watched. They too ignored him. There was no sign of the terrible Mongoose so Mel-Ca dashed across the sandy beach with his short tail under his arm.

At the water's edge he allowed the water to soak over his feet and enjoyed the splashing. Slowly, he wadded in a little distance and stood there like the Sandpipers were standing. It felt good. Soon he was moving farther out into the water, but he was riding on something. When he looked down into the clear, blue-green water he discovered he was riding on the back of a very large Leatherback Turtle. How thrilling! He swayed this way and that way until the turtle took a dive into the deeper, coral water and Mel-Ca slipped off his back. He started to bob and float. What fun! The saltwater kept him on top of the water and even helped his sore tail feel better.

Back at the zoo, Mr. Dewey looked everywhere for the missing monkey and when he discovered the unlocked gate he knew that Mel-Ca had slipped outside. He jogged through the bird sanctuary calling his name as he went. When he reached the sandy beach he looked out over the water and saw something floating in the water. He realized it was the little rascal and swam out to rescue him.

When Mel-Ca saw him he started to screech an excited, happy, short-breathy screech. Mr. Dewey swooped Mel-Ca out of the water, placed him securely on his shoulders, and swam to shore. Then he snuggled him in his arms like a baby. He noticed that part of Mel-Ca's tail was missing so he teased and tickled him." Ha, ha! Did you find trouble or did trouble find you? No more Mel-Ca running away! No more Mel-Ca running away!" he teased.

On their way back to the Zoo, Mr. Dewey and Mel-Ca were entertained by the evening symphony of the Whistling Tree Frogs. It was a sound that identifies the peacefulness of the island much like the sound of crickets on a summer evening anywhere. The Tree Frogs are very tiny and they live on the underside of leaves high in the trees. Unlike other frogs, they do not have webbed feet, but toes, and the young are not tadpoles but frogs. There are thousands of Tree Frogs throughout Barbados, and their symphony goes on all through the night.

Home safely at the zoo, Mee-Ca stopped screeching. She bounded down from the rocks to greet them. Mr. Dewey carefully lowered Mel-Ca into the monkey pit. Mee-Ca grabbed hold of him and hugged and hugged him. She began to chatter as she wrapped her tail around him and the two of them scampered off to the high rocks. Lots of monkey talk began. Mel-Ca tried to convince Mee-Ca that he had a great time outside the zoo, but when she saw that half of his tail was missing she did not think his adventure, or mis-adventure, was so great.

Mel-Ca would always have his shortened tail to remind him of the consequences of his misadventure, and his tail would no longer allow him to hang in odd positions whenever he felt the urge. Lucky for him, Mee-Ca was happy to carry him on her back as she swung about. She became quite the showoff. She screeched, almost in a sing-song fashion, and Mel-Ca covered his ears. She looped her tail on high branches and hung upside down, and Mel-Ca covered his eyes. They were the happiest monkeys in the zoo.

In no time, these two Green Monkeys became an added attraction for the tourists who visited the Barbados Zoo. Children were fascinated and they loved to hear Mr. Dewey tell the story of Mee-Ca and Mel-Ca and how Mel-Ca lost half of his tail. When it was permissible, he would lead the smaller children to a sandy area where they could sit on the back of a Giant Leatherback Turtle. One child at a time the turtle would take them for a very slow, short ride, of course, it was not into the ocean.

The message on Mr. Dewey's tee-shirt on those days was,

IT MATTERS NOT
WHAT YOU'VE GOT,
BUT WHAT YOU DO
WITH WHAT YOU'VE GOT !!!!!!

and right under the saying there was a picture of Mee-Ca carrying Mel-ca on her back as she hung from a tree branch by her long tail.

ERIN AND ELORA

TWO GREAT WHITE EGRETS IN TASMANIA

You've heard of "the land down under", haven't you? It's Australia, the continent south of the equator, and south of it, surrounded by water, is Tasmania. Tasmania is a beautiful island, and our story is about two Great White Egrets named Erin and Elora who lived on the island many, years ago. Of course the story is not real, but all the facts about the birds, the land, and other things are real.

On this beautiful island of rainforests, national parks and bushwalks, two Great White Egrets, Erin and Elora, are hiding in a hulling barn on a walnut farm. Their lives have been threatened.

These stately birds with stark white feathers are about three feet tall and weigh only about two pounds. Their legs are long and black and their talons are black. Their exceptionally long neck has a sort of crook in it, and when they fly they give their neck a slight "S" shape tuck, so they look rather odd. They fly slowly, almost gliding, without much flapping of their wings which span out about three feet.

Their plumes are elegant with soft curves and a delicate sheerness. These grow long on their back and hang loose and wispy, almost touching the ground. At the time of this story, in the early twentieth century, their feathers and plumes were in high demand throughout Europe and North America. Milliners, makers of ladies hats, needed the plumes for the ornate decorating of the fashionable hats of the era. It was a big industry.

Factories bought the plumes by the pound for high prices, and the Egrets were slaughtered by the thousands. It took four egrets to obtain one pound of plumes. Plume hunters stripped the flat, bulky nests and wipe out whole colonies of these peaceful birds. Egrets were placed on the endangered list.

It was late at night when the plume hunters raided the nests. They observed the stately birds preening, cleaning up their feathers, with their sharp, beaks before settling down for the night. When they were settled the plume hunters made their merciless attack. They emptied all the nests. The men stood under the trees to catch the falling birds and throw them into trucks that transported them to the next point to be stripped of their fine plumes which were then shipped to Europe and North America.

On one particular night Erin and Elora had spent a little longer time at a waterfall and arrived back at their colony just as the plume hunters were busy attacking the sleeping egrets. They did a quick about face and flew off in the darkest direction to save their lives.

They flew to the quiet, safe grounds of a dense walnut farm, to a hulling barn where the green outer covering of the walnut is removed, washed, dried graded and boxed for shipping They perched on the peak of the barn and Erin used her sharp, yellow beak to pry a shutter open just wide enough to squeeze inside, then Elora squeezed inside. At first, they stood there in the dark loft, straining their eyes to make out things around them. It was rather bare, and appeared to be a safe place to hide until they found a colony and mates who would help build a new nest.

Usually the male egret selects the nesting site. It could be in an abandoned site or a new one, depending upon the availability of suitable building materials. They construct a platform, in the crook of a tree, with long, flimsy sticks. Then it is lined by the female with fine, broad leaves. and soft ferns for comfort. It is a rather messy looking nest.

When egrets settle down to raise a family, typically, three to six eggs are laid and both male and female tend to the incubation of the eggs. They take turns sitting on them. Only two or three hatch and only one or two make it to the fledgling stage. The mortality rate is high for young egrets and the life span for the Great White Egret is about five years. Because they prefer to live close to lakes, bays, marshes and even swamps for the ready supply of fish, mollusk, crustaceans and frogs they are further endangered by the water contamination which is passed on through what they eat.

Erin and Elora fell asleep huddled in the barn. The noise of machinery awoke them at the crack of dawn. Before they made the slightest move, they waited and listened. Their strange exotic yellow eyes rolled this way and that to take in their new surroundings. They slowly got up on their feet, and stood very still.

Below them in the big barn men, many men, were coming and going, carrying ladders and boxes. Machinery was humming. No one looked up, and no one saw the visiting birds. They waited awhile.

When they pushed the shutter open with their beaks, they looked out on a magnificent grove of walnut trees. Not the ideal trees for a new nest because harvesting a walnut crop would disrupt the peaceful environment egrets enjoy in a forest. Perhaps the hulling barn would do until they found mates, but possibly all the male egrets were gone. They just didn't know.

<u>By the way ...</u> *Walnuts have been grown in Tasmania for many decades. The climate is neither too hot, nor too cold, and the soil is perfect. It is a profitable industry. Australia exports tons of walnuts in the year of their harvest, and proudly claim them to be the richest tasting in the world. That's because they are free of pesticides and chemicals.*

Erin and Elora left the barn and flew over the trees back toward their nests. When they got close to the roosting trees of their colony they looked down on the devastation. The remnants of nests were scattered all over the ground, and there was no sign of a beautiful white bird throughout the whole cluster of trees. There was no familiar sound of a cuk, cuk, cuk. There was no sound of any other birds either. They dare not descend for a closer look and they flew off toward the waterfall.

At the waterfall they stood in the shallow water waiting to grab a fish or even a frog with their long, sharp beaks. Many birds came to eat, but mostly they came to look at the surviving egrets. The beautiful Grey-Crowned Babblers were quietly looking on while contented little birds, Thornbills and Fantails, twittered as they ate close by.

The Magpie, one of Australia's most celebrated birds, could be heard close by too. It repeated over and over, "You're out! You're out!" It was Ruddy. He came closer to the egrets. Ruddy was an aggressive, robust, handsome Magpie with distinctive, glossy black and white, smooth feathers. He was known to tend to much of what was going on all around him. If the attack on the egret colony had occurred during the day, Ruddy and his flock would have inflicted serious injuries to the heads, necks , faces and eyes of the hunters. They have a dangerous attacking nature.

Their habit of attacking humans, especially those in motion, was scary. They'd swoop down from behind a person and peck at the head. Visitors to Australia are warned and given safe guards to protect their heads. So the famous songbird of Australia is also considered a pest. Even so, the country is proud of their talented Magpie that mimics over thirty-five species of birds, also dogs, horses, musical instruments and of course human voices.

Ruddy was aware of what happened to the egret colony and stood closer to the mourning egrets. He stood there blinking his red eyes in a most understanding way to make his friendship known to the always sociable egrets. Erin and Elora could not ignore his kindness. They rolled their exotic eyes in a quiet response. Their strange, yellow eyes rolled around in an unusual way, slightly rotating outside of their eye sockets. This looked weird, but it gave them a binocular- like vision, very important while flying.

Beyond the waterfall and the bushwalks, where visitors loved to take sight-seeing tours, something new was taking place. Baseball. Ruddy was aware that new baseball parks were being built in Tasmania. One of them was just beyond the waterfall. For the most part the Magpies were on their best behavior for baseball. They did not disturb the players or the spectators. The crowds were too intimidating for Ruddy and his flock. The Magpies were so visible that they became the favored mascots for several teams who adopted their popular colors of mostly black on white or mostly white on black uniforms. The crowds were amused with their mimic of the umpire, "You're out! You're out!" as the birds strutted around on the ball park walls.

Ruddy was aware of something else. He knew that several egrets had escaped the massacre and found a safe haven beyond the baseball park. Somehow he had to get that news across to Erin and Elora. He had a plan. He began to jabber and whistle, but he made no sense to the egrets. Then he began to mimic the "Cuk, cuk, cuk" of egrets. He still made no sense as he walked around the egrets singing their sound and blinking his red eyes at them. Their yellow eyes roll around and protruded as they watched him in dismay. They knew full well that Ruddy was not an egret.

Several Magpies gathered, and formed a line behind Ruddy as he took off over the waterfall. Then they turned around and came back to the stunned egrets. The Magpies made three trips back and forth until the egrets decided to follow the Magpies over the waterfall.

Once on the ground, Ruddy led his flock on foot into the woods. They all began to sing out "Cuk, cuk, cuk. Cuk, cuk, cuk. Cuk, cuk, cuk!" and the egrets followed in a trusting way. Then as quickly as the Magpies began to sing, they stopped, turned around, and flew off back over the waterfall. There mission was completed. The egrets were on there own now to discover the good news that Ruddy led them to.

It was quiet except for the pleasant rhythmic twitter and tweet, and soft whistles of the birds nesting in the trees. Suddenly, Erin and Elora looked at each other when they heard familiar Cuk, cuk, cuk, of real egrets. Without hesitation they flew off in the direction of the bird call.

Sure enough, they found the other egret survivors. They had started to form another colony with some Great Blue Herons and some Snowy Egrets. This was not unheard of for the Great White Egrets. They have been known to cohabitate with other species of egrets, being the social bird that they are.

They were greeted with much warmth and fussing. Erin and Elora would not have to fly back to the walnut hulling barn tonight, or any other night. Immediately, they began to preen their beautiful feathers and the "Cuk, cuk, cuk. Cuk, cuk, cuk" of happy egrets could be heard throughout the woods.

The Great White Egrets are no longer killed for their plumes. That practice has been declared illegal. Fancy hats with plumes are no longer in fashion so the egret's are starting to populate again in safety. However, there is still much contamination in the rivers and streams that birds and other animals drink out of and that fish and other animals live in. Life is a precious thing for all of God's creatures. It is good to defend, protect and preserve it.

PIP PERRI PANDA OF CHINA

This story takes place in one of the many large bamboo forests in China. It is a cold, sometimes snowy, always damp, misty place suitable for growing bamboo trees. There are over fifty different kinds of bamboo, and many uses for it today. Besides being food for the panda bears, the trees are used for building products for homes, for making fine furniture, for weaving a superior quality material for bedding and clothing, and for window coverings.

This bamboo forest is the home of giant panda bears who rely upon bamboo for their main food. The pandas roam about freely but not in total safety. Pandas are among the most endangered species in the world. Even though there are laws against poachers, illegal hunters, the pandas are still hunted and killed for their fur which sells for over one hundred thousand dollars for each bear.

Hundreds of years ago it was thought that pandas possessed some sort of magical powers. The Chinese Emperors sought them as pets for their palace. The Emperor's guards were usually on a mission to find a suitable panda for the palace. It had to be a panda with an unusual quality.

Pip Perri was a carefree two year old panda who weighed only five ounces at birth and had grown to be a chubby, pleasant looking bear. He had a large, white furry head, round black ears and black rings around his small, sharp eyes. These black rings did two things. They gave the appearance that he had large eyes, but he didn't, and they made him look sad, but he wasn't. His body was covered with beautiful, soft, thick, white fur and his legs and hind quarters were black. This little guy ate close to forty pounds of bamboo everyday, and it took him twelve to sixteen hours to do that. Pandas do not hibernate like other bears because their bodies cannot store food. So Pip Perri was a twelve month consumer of bamboo, and he loved it. He also loved to wander and discover things. He was not content with the boring existence of the usual wild giant pandas .

His curious nature discovered a beehive once and he spent hours playing a swatting game and dodged the bees who could never sting him. His coat was too thick. He was not attracted to the honey, but he just loved aggravating the bees. Oh, he loved wild flowers too. First he pulled the petals off one at a time. Then he'd eat the center and allow the stem to dangle from the side of his mouth. He was a bit odd.

One day he pushed a huge rock over and it began to roll down a steep hill. He began to tumble down too, somersault after somersault. With loud grunts, squeals and squeaks he rolled all the way to the bottom. When the rock stopped so did Pip Perri and the hill was high above him. He wanted to roll down the hill again and he started to climb up, but it was not like climbing a tree. His twelve claws were sharp, he had extra thumbs, called pseudo thumbs, for gripping bamboo, but he could not hold on to the wet, grassy soil. He kept slipping and sliding down. Finally, he fell backwards and hit his head on the big rock.

While he lay on the ground all woozy, he looked up and watched the puffy clouds spinning and bumping together. He reached up to swat at them but they were too far away. He rolled over and pushed with his chubby, short legs to get up, but kept on falling to the ground. He was so wobbly that he quit trying. He rolled himself up into a ball, a favorite position for a sleeping panda, huddled close to the rock, and went to sleep, with his sore head resting on his forearm.

It was nighttime when he awoke and looked up at the sky. The clouds were gone and in their place was a thin sliver of the moon shinning with thousands of stars in the dark sky. Nothing was spinning. Pip Perri's eyes were small with snake-like vision so he got used to the darkness all around him and could see very well in the dark. When he finally got up on all four legs, he started to walk slowly in his sideward fashion, heel toe, heel toe. Pandas do not walk upright like the Grizzly and the Polar bears. He moved toward the scent of his favorite food in a long, thick cluster of bamboo trees that grew up the side of a hill. Eagerly, he climbed up a tree to gather his meal. He carried a sweet branch down in his mouth and sat relaxing against the trunk to enjoy every leaf and sprig. He wanted more.

Even though pandas preferred to be alone, young Pip Perri missed being close to his family. He climbed back up the tree, and, then decided to climb from tree to tree. This he had never done before, but he had seen his brothers climb from tree to tree. He was sure he could do it too. His plan was to reach the top of the hill in this way, and, of course, to eat all the way.

As he climbed and feasted on pounds of chewy bamboo he took time out to peek up at the twinkling stars and sliver of a moon. It was then that he heard odd sounds far below him. When he looked down through the branches he saw two men setting traps and covering them with the conifer needles that covered the forest floor. He had never seen people before and he sensed danger.

Something he had never experienced came over him. He felt like he had to hide. So he clung to the strong branches and remained very quiet until he could no longer hear the strange noises. He looked down and watched the men walk away and out of sight. Then he started eating again and continued traveling from tree to tree until he could go no further. He had reached the top of the hill.

It was dawn when he climbed down very slowly, stopping frequently to peek through the dense, damp fog. Suddenly, where the sunlight was breaking through the trees, he saw the two men sitting on the ground pulling on ropes. Once again he sensed danger. It gave him the shivers. So he kept his eyes on the men as he turned and began to walk slowly in his sideward fashion, heel toe, heel toe, back to the bamboo trees.

He got a good grip on a tree and climbed high to safety where he could vaguely see the strangers but they could not see him. His coloring was perfect camouflage and so were all of the leaves that clung to his damp fur. Pip Perri was very patient and he would wait for as long as he had to before he would venture down again. He continued eating. He ate sprigs and all and took short snoozes while sitting astride the stronger branches. It's so easy for pandas to get comfortable. He spent another night in the forest.

At dawn nothing was moving down below. Pip Perri backed down ever so slowly. With his feet securely on the ground, he decided which way to go to find home. He recognized a huge stump of a tree that he clawed at while practicing his grip just a year ago. He picked up the familiar scent of family, and moved much faster, heel toe, heel toe in that direction.

His family, in the meantime, picked up his scent. He and they ambled about sniffing and grunting until they saw each other. His mother and two brothers just stared at him. His head looked larger with the big bump growing through the fur. Many bamboo leaves clung to his oily fur and his mouth looked weird, swollen and bloody. Mother Panda grabbed his head to examine it as she brushed the leaves off. Pip Perri gave a hurtful growl and nuzzled closer to her. Then she opened his swollen mouth and looked inside. She put her snoot inside his mouth and rubbed it over his swollen gums. Pip Perri didn't seem to mind at all. She discovered that he had lost all of his baby teeth while eating too much rough bamboo. She gave him a long hug and they sat there humming.

His permanent teeth will soon grow in and by the time he turns five he will be considered an adult. As an adult Pip Perri will be about six feet long, not tall because pandas are not considered tall. Remember they do not walk upright like other bears. He should weigh close to three hundred pounds, and if he is lucky he will live to be about twenty five years old. If he is unlucky the poachers will take his life and sell his beautiful fur. If the bamboo forest continues to become depleted, for the sake of industry, there will be no food for him. His fate looks sad and poor.

Pip Perri was about to share his great adventure with his family, but they stopped paying attention to him. They went off to be alone, to get back to eating bamboo and any small animals, birds, snakes and bamboo rats that came their way. That's just the way it is with wild pandas. Their behavior is pretty boring, whereas Pip Perri was different. He had a sense of adventure, curiosity and an unusual, light hearted attitude.

It was springtime and there was much new bamboo growing around the tree trunks. He found the low fast growing fan bamboo which was loaded with soft sweet leaves. For several days he ate to his heart's content, but gradually he got that ho-hum, panda feeling of being bored. Each day he wandered a little further away from his family again to find another adventure, and more bamboo.

Before long he arrived at the cool mountain stream that ran through the Chengdu Bamboo Forest. The banks of the stream were loaded with young plants and he continued eating and roaming along the edge of the stream. At one point Pip Perri leaned over to take a drink of the cold, bubbling water, and he toppled into the moving stream.

He rolled over and tried to get up, but the slippery rocks kept him slip sliding down and the stream moved him along. He went with the gentle flow. Not only did he find it was easier than walking, he discovered that he was a good swimmer. Pandas swim like dogs with their head held out of the water. It was effortless.

Where the stream took a bend there was a large branch hanging over the water and Pip Perri grabbed hold of it before being carried any further. The branch broke, but he fell closer to the shore and managed to get up without falling down. Finally, on solid ground again, he walked sideward, heel toe, heel toe, and shook the shiny beads of water from his fur. There is much oil under the panda's fur to protect the skin from the cool damp climate so his fur was going to remain wet for awhile.

He was in a new part of a forest of really, tall bamboo trees and his strong claws dug into the trunk of one. He hugged it and made his climb for the best food in the whole world. He made himself comfortable eating to his hearts content. When it was almost dusk, and his stomach was full, he climbed down, rolled himself up on the ground, close to the trunk of the tree, and with his head resting on his forearm, went into a deep, deep, sleep.

In the still, dark, and damp coolness of the morning he was awakened by sounds he had heard once before. They were the voices of men. He saw where they were, sensed the go hide feeling of danger again and climbed up the tree. He stayed clinging up there, waiting and munching until it was quiet below him.

These men though were there to foil, (to mess up) the traps and snares that poachers had set. They were from a habitat and their job was also to rescue any giant pandas that might get caught and injured, and take them to a safe place. When he did venture down he was startled when the men quickly threw a net over him, slid a cart with wheels under him, pulled him away, and loaded him into a truck. The doors closed with a shuddering bang! bang! and the truck started moving over a rough road of gullies and grooves.

Pip Perri was scared, trembling scared, but when his eyes adjusted to the darkness in the truck, he could make out a large shadow of something huddled in a corner, and he sensed a familiar smell. He grunted. Then he heard grunts and more grunts, familiar grunts. He rolled closer to the sounds and sure enough his brothers were in nets too. In their own bear talk way they scolded him because they had gone looking for him and lost his scent at the stream. That's where they got caught in poachers' nets. He squeaked and bleated that he had found the stream and gone for a swim. They didn't care, not one bit, and they jabbered away until the truck came to a jolting stop.

The men were surprised to find happy pandas when they opened the doors, but for safety's sake they did have to sedate them with a harmless stun-gun, because once they were released from the nets they could be angry and aggressive. They were transported on open flatbed carts to the Research Habitat Center where there were many other pandas, who had been rescued. They were climbing trees in a dense bamboo forest. The air was filled with grunts, squeaks, and hums, and there was a peacefulness in the air.

While the three pandas were still stunned, groups of doctors and scientist examined them. They listened to their hearts, looked into their eyes, ears, and mouths, and examined their limbs for injuries. When they looked into Pip Perri's mouth they felt his tummy right away and did lots of talking. Soon they had him sitting in the midst of fresh, young bamboo shoots and when he came to, he knew what to do. His brothers were released into the habitat forest where they could have their daily fill of bamboo in safety.

The giant pandas are among today's most endangered species. Poachers, as well as a depleting growth of bamboo forest, and a low birth rate have reduced the species to about only two thousand worldwide. The Chinese government did not want to loose their most treasured resource so they have built over forty habitats to protect the current panda population. This particular Natural Reserve Habitat is about eight hundred square miles, which is a pretty big area. Here the captive pandas are raised and bred to increase their numbers. Those injured by poacher traps are nursed back to good health. Some are then released back into the wild. The Habitats are a safe haven where good things are happening for pandas, for the environment, and for China.

Lan Fu, a young, woman scientist at the Natural Reserve, was the first one to notice and chart Pip Perri's behavior. She watched him amuse himself with things around him, things that other pandas ignored. He studied, pulled apart and ate flowers and plants; played an amusing game with beehives; even trapped them in buckets that were left on paths for the maintenance people. He followed a trail of ants, swept them into mounds with his paws and watched them escape in different directions. The most surprising thing though was that he managed to make other pandas laugh. A panda laughing is like watching a cat yawn with a wide open mouth, making a squeaking sound like hiccups. Can you imagine the sounds of several pandas laughing? She was amazed. Of course Lan Fu, considered him to be a Rare Bear, perhaps just what the Emperor was looking for. She contacted the Emperor's Guard, Li Chun-mo, and read all her notes about

Pip Perri to him. He was likewise impressed. Immediately they made plans for Pip Perri to be transported to the Emperor's Palace.

A message from the Imperial Office had just gone out through the land that the Empress, Yan Lun, was very ill. The people were concerned. Of equal concern was the well being of their tiny princess, Ya Ya, which means beautiful little girl. She was not eating well and cried daily because she and her mother used to spend hours together everyday and now Ya Ya felt lost. Thus, the Emperor, Mei Gao Shan, was searching for the Rare Panda Bear that would bring good spirits back to his household. He believed in the ancient Chinese lore that the Giant Pandas were mystical even magical and capable of warding off evil spirits. The time had come for Pip Perri's real test.

Now, at the Palace there was a beautiful Imperial Garden. On one side extending from the south end to the north end of the garden was a healthy bamboo forest. It was grown specifically for the panda bears that were often brought to the Palace for the test. Only a tall, thorny hedge separated the bamboo forest from the garden. Pip Perri was brought to this forest. It was up to the Emperor to decide if Pip Perri possessed magic or what is called lingji which is inspiration, sudden inspiration. Translated ling means soul and ji has many meanings including being flexible. Was Pip Perri a flexible soul? Did he possess lingji? Was he the Rare Panda Bear that the Emperor was looking for? If he was magical, in what way could he be?

Pip Perri could see the garden through small openings in the tall, thorny hedge that separated the bamboo forest from the garden. He watched the guard carry Ya Ya into the garden. Everyday they walked to a different part of the garden. One day the guard allowed Ya Ya to wander among the flowers to pick a bouquet for her mother. While she was picking the flowers butterflies fluttered above her head. Li Chun-mo gave her a net to catch one. She chased after one that flew over the hedge and landed near Pip Perri where he sat looking in at her. He swept it up and stared at it. As he thought about taking it apart like a flower, he saw the beautiful Ya Ya peeking through the hedge at him. He passed the butterfly through the small opening in the hedge to Ya Ya., and watched her run back to her guard and tell him about the panda on the other side of the hedge.

People believed the butterfly to be a symbol of new life and right away Ya Ya's life started to change. She ate that day and the next and the next, and the crying stopped. She could hardly wait to go to the garden and peek at the panda that peeked back at her. The bouquet, the butterfly and Ya Ya's excitement brought a blush to the cheeks of the Empress. She too had started to heal.

One day while Pip Perri waited for Ya Ya to arrive in the garden he caught a glimpse of her walking on the marble bridge that stretched across the center of the garden and over the still waters of the garden lake. The guard did no see her little body slip though the columns on the bridge, but Pip Perri did. He got that sudden sense of danger that he had experienced for his own life only now he sensed it for Ya Ya's life. He was not going to hide this time.

Perhaps it was that lingji, that sudden inspiration. Whatever it was, Pip Perri charged through the thorny hedge into the garden. His fur was torn from many places on his body including his head, but he pounded his paws on the ground in a fast sideward trot toward the lake. He toppled into the water head first and began to swim toward the drowning princess. He swatted his arms around in the water like he did when he swatted at the bees. Under water Ya Ya's tiny hands grabbed hold of him and he lifted her to his head where she hung on with her skinny arms and legs. Her hands clutched the fur on his forehead. Pip Perri paddled toward the guard who was also in the water now. He lifted Ya Ya off his head and handed her to the guard, who then quickly swam to shore with her.

Pip Perri remained in the water, with his large head looking out at the commotion in the garden. Then he found his way back through the hedge and tore even more fur from his body as he pushed himself through the merciless thorns. The only pain he felt though, was a sadness, a lonely emptiness, because he did not understand all that had just happened. He went to sleep moaning, hurt and hungry, wet and confused.

Early the next day the Emperor, Mei Gao Shan, came into the Imperial bamboo forest to find Pip Perri. He had to see the marvelous, heroic panda with lingji, the panda that brought joy to his household and saved the life of his beautiful little girl. His aide followed him carrying a jeweled wreath type of crown on a white satin pillow.

Pip Perri was rolled up on the ground. He opened one eye and looked up at the Emperor in his shiny, red silk robe with gold trim. The Emperor was beaming with praise for him. Mei Gao Shan looked down at Pip Perri and was quite sure he had never seen such a shaggy, sad looking panda. This panda with tufts of fur missing from his head, shoulders and limbs, and thorns tangled in his wet, matted fur, looked pathetic. Immediately though, the Emperor sensed this panda bear had a heroic greatness, a mystical, magical greatness found only in the Rare Panda Bear with lingji. He reached for the jeweled wreath type of crown and placed it on Pip Perri's head. The bear was weak from the hunger and shock. He could not move. The Emperor spoke in loud strange sounds which Pip Perri did not understand. Pip Perri did sense something good had happened though. It must be something good that pleased the Emperor because the Emperor held his arms out toward Pip Perri with his palms up, and he raised his arms high in the air as he continued to speak on and on.

Pip Perri sensed no fear. He had a good feeling. He sat up and reached up to touch the thing on his head. He removed it and stared at the beauty of it. Somehow he knew it was not to be pulled apart or eaten. He carefully pressed it back on his head. Then he bowed his head to the Emperor and his aide. It was another sudden inspiration thing. They starred at this rare bear with lingji. They were impressed.

Pip Perri went on living in the Imperial Palace Garden long after he was twenty-five years old. In fact, he was considered a valuable member of the Emperor's family. He was included in all the special parades, and wore his crown. He would sit in a huge pile of bamboo leaves on a parade cart, and eat as the happy people waved at him along the parade route. All of China knew that the rarest panda ever found was Pip Perri.

Ya Ya grew up talking and walking with Pip Perri in the Imperial Garden. He grew to an enormous size and his gentleness also grew. They made each other laugh often. Of course, his laugh made her laugh even more. Pip Perri was blessed with much lingji, and the Imperial Family felt blessed too.

ZIP ZAP A YOUNG ZEBRA IN KENYA

The usual months of March through May brought very little rain to Kenya in East Africa. The earth was dry and dusty, and the scrub growth of grasses and bushes had started to curl for want of water. Fortunately, the Samburu Forest, in the heartland of Kenya, proved to be a comfortable shelter for a most important event in mid-September.

A stately, zebra stallion stood at the edge of the forest with his harem of five mares and four foals. He waited watchfully. His round, cone shaped ears were tilted forward ready to pick up the familiar sound of another one of his mares. His three year old mare had gone into the forest to be alone. One year and forty-one days were completed and she was ready to deliver her first born foal. Her stallion and his harem stood a goodly distance away waiting for the delivery, and they guarded the area near the open forest.

The Grevy's stallion is the largest of all zebras. He is five feet tall at the shoulder and his body is eight feet long. He is a powerful protector weighing over nine hundred pounds.

When the mare's whinnying and loud snorting breaths stopped, the stallion leaned his head forward. He waited and listened for the familiar sound of faint snorts of a new foal. When he heard them he nodded to the harem and they proceeded into the forest for the first look at the newborn foal. The stallion remained on guard, ever watchful for the zebra enemies who roamed throughout the forest. There were enemies who could and would attack at any moment. Enemies who would go for the weakest, slowest zebra in the harem, a new born foal.

Immediately after the birth, the mother mare stood up and encouraged her baby to stand and test his legs. It usually takes a foal close to half an hour to do this and then about another half hour to run about. This feisty little guy hit the ground running. Right away he showed signs of strength and he appeared to be unusually sure of himself.

The harem formed a circle around the mother and her foal. They watched him prance back and forth as if he was doing a dance. His legs were long and his eight-five pound body made him appear old already.

He was not white with black stripes like the rest of the zebras, but was white with reddish-brown colored stripes, and a dark mane. It stood straight up, and extended from his head and down the length of his back to the base of his tail. This was Zip Zap, the youngest member of a Grevy's zebra harem. Currently, the Grevy's species has dwindled to fewer than 2,500 in the world, and is on the endangered list.

By the time Zip Zap is a year old he will leave the harem to join up with a male herd. It is nature's plan that the young zebras learn the ways of the species. For when the right day comes, and he is ready, he will challenge a stallion for the ownership of his harem. There'll be a battle of strengths and there will be one winner. One stallion controls a harem of several mares.

While Zip Zap does not yet resemble the grand looks of the Grevy's zebra, his reddish-brown stripes will gradually turn to thin black stripes on his white body. The stripes will wrap around his legs, back and hind quarters, but not around his belly, that will remain white. The white belly distinguishes the Grevy's from the Burchell's zebra. No two zebras have identical stripes. Their stripes are their identity marks like our finger prints are ours. Zip Zap had an artistic pattern of black, diamond shaped stripes from his forehead to the tip of his nose. He had wide open, black eyes and was alert and handsome.

Suddenly, the stallion arrived at the circle and gave out a danger warning, a coarse, braying sound. His large lips quivered showing his teeth and he trotted around the rim of the circle to herd the harem out of the forest. They took off in a gallop into the vast semi-arid desert. They knew there was some threat of danger. The last to join the harem was Zip Zap and his mother. She didn't feel like racing, but Zip Zap was ready for anything. He zipped past her. The stallion stood up on his hind legs, whinnied loudly, to insist they race even faster for the pounding paws of a hungry young, spotted cheetah, who dropped from a tree, kicked up dust as it raced after the harem. The cheetah, known to be the fastest of the African cats, can out race lions, leopards, and zebras, but not on this day.

The stallion reared up on his front legs, came down swiftly and caught the cheetah's small head with both hind hooves. The cheetah was badly wounded by the powerful hooves of the stallion. He hissed and screeched loudly, fell on his back and struggled to get back on his feet. Quickly, the stallion came down upon his chest with his strong front legs. The cheetah drew his last breath and laid harmless on the dry earth.

Zip Zap stopped running when he heard the screeching cheetah sounds. He turned around and saw how his father defended the harem from a deadly enemy. He saw how the great stallion saved his harem and new born son for a better day with one less enemy. Then he galloped off to join up with the harem where they stood at the edge a Lake Barango for a refreshing drink.

The great stallion stood off a short distance, with watchful eyes, for he knew that this wide open space was ideal for another enemy to pounce upon a member of his family. He also knew that before long the cowardly hyena clan would find the body of the dead cheetah and begin to feast upon it.

Zip Zap heard the outrageous laugh of the hyena which is always heard when there is food present. It is actually a call to other clan members to come and eat and can be heard for several miles. His father motioned to him to come to his side. He did. They trotted off a short distance together where they could watch the hyenas devour the entire cheetah, flesh, bones, and hooves, even hair. There was only a red spot left on the ground when they were finish. They are true scavengers. Their faces are white because they eat the bones of animals. The ugly, haunch back animals, with short hind legs crept off in different directions smacking their lips and making satisfied grunts and burps.

Zip Zap looked up at his father for an answer to the question in his young eyes. "What was that all about?"

The great stallion looked down and starred into his eyes, "Survival", was his answer, and he nudged him to return to his mother.

She was waiting for him and he realized that he could pick her out from the other zebras because he knew her scent. He was happy. Immediately, he started to nurse like a one day old baby is supposed to do. The little guy learned much on his first day of life.

That night when they settled down to rest for the night they were hidden by thorny dry shrubs. Zebras sleep standing up and there is always one or two who stand guard to warn the harem of approaching danger. Still, the giant shadow of the great stallion appeared in the distance.

In the morning a tourist safari came traveling in a long, white and black stripped van, and stirred up fumes with the dust. The zebras looked up from their grazing. Zip Zap wandered toward the van. To him it was a strange zebra, a very strange zebra.

Zip Zap saw his father and galloped away from the fumes of the van toward his father. He looked up at him and could tell he was acting different. His nostrils were making a puffing sound and his eyes were wide. "What?" the foal begged in innocence.

The stallion bumped his nose on Zip Zap's rump. Again he begged "What?" This time he received a bump so hard that it moved Zip Zap forward. He did it again until the foal got the message and dashed off to find his mother. He sensed he should not stray away from the harem.

The guide stopped the van and began, "Ladies and gentlemen, these are Grevy's zebras, they are on the endangered list. The young are always the object of attack by the meat eating wild animals, lions, leopards, cheetahs, and hyenas, that live throughout this area. These preditiors, plus poor grazing, because of livestock, cattle, sheep and goats, because of poachers, and even these safari trips, all contribute to the Grevy's being endangered." The van rolled slowly on down the dusty road while the tourists snapped pictures of the zebras.

When the light rains of December started and would not stop, the harem traveled off to higher land to the south trudging slowly through the cool rain that created streams flowing through the desert ruts and gullies. The slush reached their ankles until they arrived at the grassy, foothills of Mt. Kenya where they took shelter for the night under some flat-top Acacia Umbrella trees. They are the national tree of Kenya.

Zip Zap looked up the side of the mountain where there were holes like small caves. His attention was drawn to one such hole. He slowly climbed closer and determined that there was a head and a leg of an animal protruding from the hole. The animal was a hyena, a young hyena. His head appeared to dangle and his leg also looked limp. He looked weak and trapped. He was exhausted from trying to break loose. Zip Zap felt compelled to help him.

He picked up a tree branch with his teeth and reached it up to the hyena's mouth. At first the hyena was afraid and moved his head to the side, but as Zip Zap insisted he finally grabbed the branch with his teeth. Even a young hyena possesses large, strong teeth that are called bone-crushers. In fact, hyenas were once thought to have jaws more powerful than any other carnivorous mammal.

The hyena clutched the branch tightly while Zip Zap tugged on the other end with all his might. The hyena popped out of the hole and took a tumble down the hillside. Zip Zap followed and landed on his rump next to the hyena. Both were bewildered as they sat there looking at each other. Then Zip Zap noticed that the hyena was missing one of his hind legs. He was exhausted so he laid down next to the hyena and went to sleep.

When Zip Zap awoke in the early dawn, the hyena was resting his head on him and was snoring. The hyena stood and fell, stood and fell. He had no balance and he could not walk, so Zip Zap crouched down next to him, very close. He nudged and nudged the weak hyena to climb upon his back. Finally, he did and clung to Zip Zap's thick mane. They joined the harem on their trek toward the grazing land of the Samburu Village.

Two young, native boys, Alder and Aulpo, who were tending sheep, spotted the strange sight of the zebra with a hyena on his back. They approached cautiously. The taller and older boy, Alder, said, "The zebra wants us to take the hyena."

"How do you know?" asked Aulpo, the younger boy.

"Because he stands there so still, looking into my eyes, saying, "Help.""

"The hyena is evil," insisted the Aulpo. "They love to attack our sheep."

"Maybe so," replied Alder. "But this hyena has only three legs. He is an outcast to his clan. He could be of use to us."

"But how?" asked the serious Aulpo. "His laugh will draw other hyenas and they could easily destroy our herd."

"I have heard that the hyena has two sides. He brings light or darkness to his surroundings. If he is treated kindly he will bring us light," said Alder. "I'm not sure how though"

"Are you sure? I have never heard that before," questioned Aulpo.

"Come, we will take this hyena to Papa Ta. He will tell us what is right." said Alder.

They lifted the hyena from Zip Zap's back. He gave no resistance. "Oh my! Only three legs. I don't know what good he can be to us," insisted the Aulpo.

"That's a good sign. No other hyena will come near him," replied Alder. "And they won't come near our land or our herd either."

Zip Zap looked after the boys as they carried the hyena away with them. Then he turned and trotted off to his mother who stood at the back of the harem waiting for her exceptional son to join her.

Papa Ta was a very tall, thin, dark old man with white tufts of hair all over his head. He was the grand father of the boys. He stood outside his multi-family hut which was built from the bark of coconut trees. The flat roof was thatched with coconut leaves and a colorful woven blanket hung across the doorway into the hut.

"Look, here, Papa Ta," said Alder. A zebra brought this hyena to us. He carried him on his back. What can you tell us about this animal? Can he be of use to us?"

Papa Ta reached down to touch the hyena's head, to look into his eyes, and to examine his hind quarters. "He is weak," he began slowly in a deep voice. "He has been abandoned because he is deformed. He is grateful to be saved. His eyes are begging to be accepted. His stomach is very empty and he has no strength in the one hind leg that he has."

"Is he of any use to us?" the two boys asked, in one voice.

"All of God's creatures have a use," Papa Ta replied. "We can make him strong and train him to herd our sheep. The hyena is an intelligent, trainable animal. But he must only be taught kindness. We won't know until we give him some of our food if he is going to use the laughter that attracts other hyenas. He is so young we can teach him our ways. We will know more about his future by how he takes to our food. Take him to the women."

The boys carried the hyena behind the hut where the women were preparing *posho*, a native meal made from corn (or maize) which is ground into flour. The *posho*, also called *ugali*, is a porridge. The women were adding mashed beans and potatoes to the large pot on the open fire, and mixed it with a long handled spoon.

"Papa Ta said to give this hyena some of our food," Alder said to the women. "We are going to train him to herd the sheep. But first we need to feed him."

"Does he have a name?" asked one of the women.

"I think I would like to call him Ugo," said Aulpo, "and when I have to tend to the sheep I will say to him, "Ugo!" And he will obey if we train him right. That's what Papa Ta said." The women laughed loudly.

Alder placed the hyena down in front of a bowl of warm *posho*. The hyena looked at those watching him and did not utter one sound. This was his first meal ever. He had not learned about calling out to others to come and eat, or how to capture food. He was hungry and being fed so he ate every morsel. He licked the bowl clean and then smacked his lips.

"This is a good sign that he is ready to be trained in the ways of the Samburu people," said Alder. The boys looked at each other with broad smiles.

"Now we must teach him how to walk."

"Good ," said Aulpo. "Papa Ta will tell us how to do that."

Papa Ta was watching and listening to the boys. "Here is how you will teach him to walk," he said. "Never bring his food to him. Coax him to come to his food. Always place it further and further away. He will get to it on his own strength and desire. He will force his three legs to work for him, and he will get stronger and stronger. Reward him with affection when he gets to his food each time. He will grow to trust us. He will work hard to please us for we are his new family."

"Come, let's take Ugo to meet the sheep and our sheep dog", said Alder.

"Good," said Aulpo. "May I carry him this time?"

"Of course you can," replied Alder. "Hold him close to your body like he was one of our little lambs."

Aulpo could feel Ugo's heart beating, and Ugo's eyes closed. He was not afraid any more.

Life had changed for the better for Ugo on that beautiful, rainy day in Kenya. Thanks to Zip Zap the zebra who made a difference and who was now three months old and starting to get his thin, black stripes.

CPSIA information can be obtained
at www.ICGtesting.com
Printed in the USA
LVIC042318211211
260538LV00001B